I0141948

What's being said about Awakened to Action?

"Will be a life saver for many men all over the globe if they will take heed to the message"

Bob Beaudine

Best Selling Author and President/CEO of Eastman-Beaudine

"Without action we have nothing, and Scott Tucker's book is the must have book for not just your library but your life! If you are searching to live the most fulfilled life imaginable, then the tools and exercises in *Awakened to Action* will bring your clarity to your purpose in life"

~ Tim Davis

Author, Speaker, and Trainer for The John Maxwell Team

"If you truly want to grow, you have to raise your awareness to your growth potential...and then take the inspired action to get you there. In Awakened to Action, Scott Tucker has identified the critical elements we men need to know to be fulfilled, and then gives the action steps to incorporate them into life...for the rest of our lives! Thanks for sharing the path to excellence and fulfillment!"

~ Scott Schilling

Speaker, Trainer, Business Coach and Best Selling Author

ISBN 13: 978-0-9753936-5-9
ISBN 10: 0975393650

Awakened to Action

Becoming a Godly Man in a Modern World

Scott R. Tucker

To my best friend and the love of my life, Bryn. For showing me unconditional love and encouragement in my daily journey to become the man God has called me to be.

Table of Contents

Introduction 6

Study 1: Love is about action! 9

Study 2: Respect 37

Study 3: Godly Friendships 65

Study 4: Suiting up for Battle 81

Study 5: Awakening Your Purpose 109

Additional Resources 123

Introduction

Welcome to *Awakened to Action!* I want to thank you for taking the time to invest in your walk with God. My prayer for this book is that all who read it be blessed abundantly and be empowered to step out boldly into the mission God has for your life.

The reasoning behind writing this book is quite simple. God told me to! You see, I have read a multitude of men's study books and have steadily grown in my knowledge of God's fundamentals because of them. What I wasn't getting from those books, were every day tools and action steps to help me incorporate those two thousand year old fundamentals into realistic action steps that are applicable to my life today. During a conversation with a pastor friend of mine, the words that came to me were as clear as the words my friend was speaking. "Stop complaining and waiting for someone else to do the work I am asking you to do!"

With that, I set out to write the book the Lord asked me to write! As I began writing this book, I will admit, there were numerous days that I spent almost entranced in typing. Never before had I allowed the Holy Spirit to flow through me, unimpeded, for such extended periods of time. Writing this book has been an amazing experience for me and I pray that your heart be opened and that you allow the Holy Spirit to be with you as you read it.

Before you get started, I do want to issue a slight word of caution. If you are a new believer or this is the first book that you have decided to do as part of a men's group study, this book may at times become a bit overwhelming to you. During my writing, there were two words that resounded over and over in my head. "Obnoxiously invasive" In obedience, I didn't pull any punches, nor did I sugarcoat or water down any aspect or teaching in my writing.

My goal with this book is not to make you feel good or give you a warm fuzzy when you're done reading it. My goal is to make you as uncomfortable as possible in the areas of your life that are not in alignment with God's will for you; and then give you the real world tools you need to succeed in those areas.

My brothers in Christ, It is time to wake up! It is time to take action! It is time to be accountable for who you are and the decisions you are making in your life!

~ Be Blessed

Study 1

Love is about Action!

For this portion of the book, the focus will be primarily on your relationship with your mate, and then extend the thoughts out to the other areas of your life. The reasoning for this is very simple. If you're not happy at home, you're not going to be able to maintain happiness outside of the home. As you read through these chapters, you'll notice that key attention is paid to the everyday scenarios most men will encounter. As stated in the intro, this book isn't an in-depth study of fundamentals, you are expected to know those by now; this book is about action! Let's get started.

Love her as Christ loved the church!

Recently, the senior pastor of our church said that, "any man who has to tell you he is the head of the household, isn't". If you are abiding by God's laws and are consistently being a Man of God, your leadership will be known through your actions, not by your words. You can shower your mate with words of affirmation; but if your actions contradict the words you are saying, which one do you think she is going to believe? Think about it from your own experiences when it comes to "words versus actions" with your mate. You know very well what the words "I'm fine" means. She might say it, but the fact that she won't make eye contact with you tells you a different story.

Before you read this first section, answer the following questions. If you are doing this study in a small group, do these questions out loud before you move on. Come back to this at the end of the section and review your answers. See if the answers are any different than when you started. If they are, write down the new answers below your original answers.

What is the first image that comes to mind when you think about your mate?

How do you describe your relationship with your mate to your friends?

Do you keep score of the mistakes your mate makes, or do you forgive and "forget"?

"Husbands, love your wives, just as Christ loved the church and gave himself up for her to make her holy, cleansing her by the washing with water through the word, and to present her to himself as a radiant church, without stain or wrinkle or any other blemish, but holy and blameless." ~ Ephesians 5:25-27

In order to show your mate true love, you have to be willing to love her as Christ loved the church. You have to create for yourself the image of her as radiant, without stain, wrinkle or blemish. You have to look beyond the turmoil and frustrations of your daily life and see her the way you did when you first met. You have to see her as the amazing and unblemished gem that she was on your first date. Every morning when you wake up, you have to wipe clean the happenings of yesterday. Until you do that, you are robbing her of the true love she deserves from you.

In Matthew 6, it says "Therefore do not worry about tomorrow, for tomorrow will worry about itself. Each day has enough trouble of its own". The same principle applies to yesterday as it does for tomorrow! Make a choice today to put everything that happened yesterday, last week, last month, last year behind you.

*****Action Tool:** Find a photo of when you first met your mate and take a long look at it. Take a moment to remember the care-free love and adoration you had for her back then. Then, keep it with you and look at it every day, more importantly, look at it every time you start to get frustrated with your mate. Regroup and make the choice to love and adore her like the day that photo was taken!*

****Action Step: Make a list of the top 5 reasons you fell in love with your mate! I encourage you to copy these reasons down on the back of the photo you are now going to be carrying around with you.***

1.)

2.)

3.)

4.)

5.)

What does true love look like?

What are the characteristics of love? 1 Corinthians says it best:

"Love is patient, love is kind. It does not envy, it does not boast, it is not proud. It does not dishonor others, it is not self-seeking, it is not easily angered, it keeps no record of wrongs. Love does not delight in evil but rejoices with the truth. It always protects, always trusts, always hopes, always perseveres." ~ 1 Corinthians 13:4-7

How does that translate to into action in today's world? For this study, we are going to go step by step through each of these elements. Be prepared to dig in and do some work, gentleman; you will get out of this what you are willing to put into it. If you want real improvements in your relationship, you have to be willing to be honest with yourself and your mate about your hang-ups. You can't let your ego get in the way of becoming the man that God has called each of you to be.

As you go through each step, remember something: your mate is the best accountability partner you could ever ask for, you just have to be willing to ask her to keep you accountable!

Love is Patient

Does it really matter if she needs an hour (or longer) to get ready to go out? She's preparing herself for you! One of the easiest ways to sabotage a potentially wonderful evening with your mate is to chastise her for taking too long to get ready. If being on time is that important to you, get off your butt and help with the housework/homework/kids/dinner or whatever it is that would give her the extra time she needs to get ready!

*******Action Tool:*** **Sometimes you have to learn to hit the "pause" button!**

Proverbs 14:29 ~ "Whoever is patient has great understanding, but one who is quick-tempered displays folly."

You can't allow the distractions and frustrations of your day dictate your attitude at home. Find your own "pause" button and start implementing it in your daily life. This is going to look different for everybody; don't stress about your pause button being the same as someone else's. If it works for you, do it!

***Action Step: What is your "pause" button? Write down your primary, and also write down an alternate. Trust me, you will need more than one in some circumstances! Once you have them written down, share them with your group or with your accountability partner. If they know your preferred tools, they can help you use them. (Your "pause" button can be something as simple as taking a deep breath, don't over complicate things!)*

Primary:

Alternate:

***Extension Step: Think of someone in your life, other than your mate, that has little patience with you. What is the underlying root of their constant frustration? Is it solely them, or do your actions serve as a catalyst in the situation? Write that person's name below and along with one thing you can do to diffuse the situation the next time it arises.*

Love is kind

One of my favorite quotes is "Don't do or say anything to your wife that you wouldn't want another man saying or doing to YOUR daughter." Let that sink in guys, especially if you have daughters. Don't do anything towards your mate that you wouldn't be ok with some guy doing to your daughter.

Do you yell at your mate? Talk down to her? Use curse words with her? Ignore her, slam doors, walk away from her? All of those things are complete disrespect to the woman you love and destroys her trust and safety with you. Bottom line: Stop doing it!

In Job 6:14, it says

"Anyone who withholds kindness from a friend forsakes the fear of the Almighty."

Your mate is no different from anyone else in your life. In fact, she should be your closest friend! Look at what it means, by definition, to "withhold kindness". In essence, you have made a conscious decision to "refrain from giving or granting" a "good or benevolent nature or disposition". In others words, you are forsaking the fear of the Lord because you don't want to be nice!

****Action Tool:** Kindness takes many forms. Understanding what kindness looks like in your relationship go way beyond biting your tongue and not speaking ill towards your mate. To understand what your mate perceives as kindness, I recommend reading "The 5 Love Languages" by Dr. Gary Chapman. Once you have a better understand of her perception and what makes her "tick", you'll be better able to demonstrate "Acts of Random Kindness" in your relationship.*

****Action Step: Determine your mate's primary and secondary love language and list 3 things you can do on a daily or weekly basis that she will perceive as kindness or love.***

1.)

2.)

3.)

****Extension Step: List 2 people in your life that you interact with on a daily basis. Next to their name, try to determine their love language and write down 1 thing you can do to show them an act of kindness. Keep it simple, this doesn't have to be anything extravagant.***

1.)

2.)

Love does not envy

Envy is incredibly destructive to any relationship. What does envy look like? If I can't have it, neither can you! That's envy, plain and simple.

It is never acceptable to set out to sabotage or destroy anything in your mate's life. Envy most commonly arises in a relationship when outside influences such as "things" or people are involved. A promotion at work, a friend they spend too much time with, the newer or nicer car, or just something as simple as the amount of free time they have; all of these things are examples of where envy tends to rear its head. In James 3:16, it is said that *"For where you have envy and selfish ambition, there you find disorder and every evil practice."* There is no need for competition with your mate. Be grateful for every accomplishment and every achievement they make. Always remember, envy is a negative action step that starts with jealousy.

Ecclesiastes 4:4 ~ "And I saw that all toil and all achievement spring from one person's envy of another. This too is meaningless, a chasing after the wind."

*****Action Tool: How many times have you used the expression "must be nice" or thought "What did she do to deserve that"? These kinds of comments and thoughts have no place in your relationship! God blesses everyone differently, be grateful for what you have, and don't be disgruntled about the accomplishments of your mate!***

***Action Step: We all have key phrases that we say or think that trigger a feeling of discontentment towards our mate. What are 3 "red flag" phrases in your life that you use when you feel those stirrings of jealousy and discontentment? Recognize them and remove them from your vocabulary! When you feel those emotions start to arise, instead of being negative, replace that sarcasm or discontent with a blessing over her.*

1.)

2.)

3.)

***Extension Step: List 2 people in your life that you recognize envious feelings toward. If you're not sure how to recognize these people, here are a few indicators. List the people that you have said "If we had what they have", "If I made the kind of money he/she made", "When I have as much free time as..." etc. All of these statements have an inherent negative connotation that harbors envy. Then, make a conscious decision to say a prayer of blessing over them every time you find yourself harboring those feelings.*

1.)

2.)

Love does not boast, it is not proud

In your relationship, you are on equal ground. There is nothing you can do to make you the "better" spouse! It's time to stop boasting and *stop score-boarding!* Don't mention it to her that you did laundry or housework or anything else that she would have normally done. Let her notice it! The fact that you didn't pull the classic "see what I did" is what she will remember and appreciate. There is no need to draw attention to your actions; your job is to serve each other. You don't get extra credit for doing your job!

Want to know the easy way to recognize pride in your relationship with your mate? It's called a bruised ego! Your ego is the value and importance you put on yourself, and the things you do. Where your ego, or pride, becomes a negative attribute in your relationship is when you put a higher value on something other than your mate. There is a fine line between confidence and arrogance. Make a daily effort not to overvalue the things you do in your relationship. By doing so, you are only setting yourself up for failure!

Proverbs 11:2 ~ "When pride comes, then comes disgrace, but with humility comes wisdom."

*****Action Tool: Pride is a destructive factor in any relationship. One simple tool to diminish pride is avoiding "right-fighting" with your mate. (Right-fighting is exactly what it sounds like, arguing over who is right!)***

****Action Step: What are 3 areas of your relationship with your mate in which you tend to have consistent right-fights and what can you do to diffuse the conflict when it arises? (Examples could be kids, money, household responsibilities, etc.)***

1.)

2.)

3.)

****Extension Step: List 2 people in your life, other than your mate, that you habitually end up "right-fighting" with. Next to their name, write down the emotions you feel when the argument starts and then ask yourself "when was the first time I felt this way towards him/her?" What did they do to make you so upset that you feel the need to always be right with them? Is it time to forgive them of that original transgression and let it go?***

1.)

2.)

Love does not dishonor others

This goes along well with "Love is Kind". Watch your words and watch your actions. Always remember it is what is caught, not what is taught that makes the biggest impression on your relationship.

With the exception of seeking advice from trusted spiritual council, (i.e. True friends, Pastors, Advisors, men's group), it is NEVER acceptable to talk openly about a hardship in your relationship to the general public! The guys you work with, play golf with, etc should not be privileged to the inner goings on of your relationship! First off, it's none of their business, and second, they probably don't care anyways! If you're not sure who can be included in the "o.k." to talk to list, don't fret, we will cover it later.

Speak only of how amazing your mate is to the general public. If you have nothing good to say, shut up! Every time you speak ill words about her, you are dishonoring her. Remember, the two of you are as one flesh, what you speak over her, is a reflection onto yourself!

"Sin is not ended by multiplying words, but the prudent hold their tongues." ~ Proverbs 10:19

*****Action Tool: Always remember, "It's not what's taught, it's what's caught". In any relationship where you are the leader, whether it be spiritual, physical, or otherwise, those that look up to you will do as you have set example, regardless of the words you say to them.***

*****Action Step: Identify 3 areas in your relationship with your mate in which your actions may be telling her something that is contradictory to your words. Then, write down one step you can take to correct the current behavior.***

1.)

2.)

3.)

*****Extension Step: Identify 4 people in your life that YOU have repeatedly dishonored. List the action that dishonored them and the repercussions of that action. Then, list an action you can take to begin the healing process in that relationship. Is it an apology? Is it a forgiveness issue?***

1.)

2.)

3.)

4.)

Love is not self-seeking

The minute you said "I do", your life became about we and us, not I and me! Every decision you make affects both of you. Stop being selfish! There is a scripture in the signature block of every email I send, also from 1 Corinthians, *"When I was a child, I talked like a child, I thought like a child, I reasoned like a child. When I became a man, I put the ways of childhood behind me"*. It is a daily reminder that my life is not only about me anymore. It is also about my wife and my children. Some of the most common areas of a man's life where selfishness tends to arise are quality time with their mate, personal belongings, and personal space. All three of these areas, as with most aspects of selfishness, have a common theme. The theme is possessiveness. Being possessive is a sign of selfishness in your life. It is also a clear indicator of insecurity and a lack of self confidence. In order to overcome a self-seeking attitude in your relationship, you must overcome the need to be possessive of anything in your relationship.

Proverbs 18:1 ~ An unfriendly person pursues selfish ends and against all sound judgment starts quarrels.

*****Action Tool: Find something to remind yourself of your commitment to live life as "We" instead of "Me" and put it somewhere that you will see it every day, several times a day.***

Action Step: Identify 2 areas of your relationship with your mate where possessiveness and selfishness have caused struggle for you.

1.)

2.)

**** Extension Step: Take a moment to look back to your childhood days and see if you can find the root of the reason for the areas of your life in which to tend to have a possessive nature. Was it growing up poor, in a cold or broken home, being abandoned? When did the possessive nature begin to show itself in your life? It's time to call it out into the light and seek power over it! Write your answers down below and then share them with your small group or trusted council.***

Love is not easily angered

Want to show her you love her? Take your "short fuse" and get rid of it. The reality of a relationship is that you're not always going to agree on things. Whether it be finances, parenting, or maybe even something as trivial as where to go on vacation. A few years ago, I attended a self-development training that was designed to teach you about how your life's experiences affected your life now. On the first day of the training, I earned the lovely nickname "powder keg". I was a time bomb of anger just waiting to go off on anybody who crossed my path. Many times, it was my wife that caught the brunt end of my anger. I learned something at that training that changed my world though. *"Anger isn't an emotion, it's a reaction to an underlying emotion."* Stop and look at the situations in your life that cause you to become angry. Why does it upset you so much? Look to the underlying root of the problem and find a way to deal with it! When you begin to to de-fuse your anger, you will find that patience becomes a lot easier!

*****Action Tool: Identify your emotional "hot buttons". Remember, anger is not an emotion; it is simply a reaction to an underlying emotion. If there wasn't something there to cause the reaction, you wouldn't have any buttons to push!***

Ecclesiastes 7:9 ~ "Do not be quickly provoked in your spirit, for anger resides in the lap of fools."

Action Step: What are your "hot buttons" in your relationship with your mate? These are the topics or actions that set you off almost instantaneously. Identify 3 of your "hot buttons" and describe why these things are such a powerful inflammation to you.

1.)

2.)

3.)

Extension Step: Analyze your actions in situations outside of that with your mate. When you become angry, how do you deal with the situation? Are your actions more subdued or are they stronger? Do you show more restraint with the outside world than you do with your mate; or do you lash out at them to "make up" for the restraint you show at home? Take the rest of this page to journal your answers .

Love keeps no record of wrongs

No more score-boarding! That's the bottom line! There are many of us that have had to say at one point or another, "I'm not who I used to be". Everyone makes mistakes, everyone has a bad day from time to time; there is nothing you can do to stop it. Your mate is not any different. What you can stop, is holding it over your mate's head! If I can recommend any one particular aspect of love to work on first and foremost in your relationship, this would be it! Yesterday is gone, let it go. This morning is gone, let it go. The argument ten minutes ago is done, let it go! Every single day of your life, Christ has to forgive you for the mistakes you make. He paid the ultimate price so that we may be deemed worthy in the eyes of God the father. Show your mate the same love Christ shows you!

Leviticus 19:18 ~ "Do not seek revenge or bear a grudge against anyone among your people, but love your neighbor as yourself."

*****Action Tool: As my dear friend and relationship mentor Amy Ensminger would (and still regularly does) say........."PUT THE CHALK DOWN!" Make a conscious effort every day to put the past behind you and start each day with a clean slate.***

***Action Step: Identify 3 things that have happened in your relationship with your mate; things you hold on to and hold against her. If you've ever tried to gain leverage or turn the tide in an argument with the words, "remember when you….." that is a good example of score-boarding, write it down! Right now is your chance to finally get it out one last time, and truly give your mate the forgiveness she deserves. Then, ask God to forgive you for your unwillingness to forgive your mate and lift up her transgressions up to him. Once you've truly given it to God, you can't get it back, so if you're not in place to truly let go of something, leave a place to come back and fill it in later.*

1.)

2.)

3.)

***Extension Step: Who else in your life are still holding a grudge against? Write their name in the space below and then start spending time in prayer about the proper steps you need to take in order to forgive them. You have to rest of the page to journal on, so fill it up if you need to.*

Love does not delight in evil, but rejoices with the truth

What does it mean to delight in evil in your relationship with your mate? Have you ever uttered the words, "Serves you right", "that's what you get", "you brought in on yourself", "you got what you deserved".......I could keep going, but you get the point. All of these statements are taking delight in evil. You should NEVER stand against your mate when something goes wrong in her life! Regardless of the situation, it is your job to stand by her side and support her! You know, "....for better or worse, richer or poorer..." any of that ring a bell? You took an oath, or one day will, to be there beside her no matter what. Do it! When you make that commitment to yourself, you find your own unique way to rejoice in Truth! If you're not there for her in the bad times, you may not be around to see the good times!

Proverbs 12:19 ~ "Truthful lips endure forever, but a lying tongue lasts only a moment."

*****Action Tool: When your mate is met with a failure or life lesson, be supportive to her and affirm her. Do whatever is needed to assure her that you are going to stand beside her through her struggles. It is not an act of sympathy to do this; it is taking an action of supporting her in the way that has been asked of you as a spiritual leader and man of God!***

****Action Step: Ask your mate for 3 areas of her life that she feels you are not supportive in her efforts and struggles. Regardless of her answers, write them down and DO NOT get defensive! This is not the time for a "right-fight"; it is a chance for you to give her a safe place to give you feedback.***

1.)

2.)

3.)

****Extension step: Identify 3 other people in your life that count on you for affirmation and leadership in their lives. Ask them the same question you asked your mate. Write their names and responses in the spaces below.***

1.)

2.)

3.)

Love always protects, always trusts, always hopes, always perseveres

The key word in this passage is "always". I talk about the aspect of protecting your mate in the "respect" study, so for now let's focus on trust, hope, and persevere. Trust is very simple. Don't second guess your mate. If she tells you something, believe it and take it to heart. There is no room in a relationship for a "prove it" mentality. Trust is a no-strings-attached agreement. One thing you have to understand, is that trust in normal relationships may be hard to earn and easy to lose, but in the relationship between you and your mate, normal rules need not apply.

Hope very simply, is not focusing on the negative in your relationship. Are you willing to always see the positive things that are happening and make the choice to focus on them? Do you have what it takes to tell her "No matter what happens, WE are going to get through this!" and truly mean it? Hope means that the "D" word is NEVER discussed in your relationship. You're never "just done" or "fed up" when it comes to your mate. You made a commitment, and you are going to find a way, together, to make it through the tough times!

When you put all of these other aspects of love into action, perseverance just happens. When you have dedicated yourself to loving your mate unconditionally, success becomes the norm. Once you have made the choice to truly love your mate the way Christ loves you, there is no possible outcome for your relationship other than to persevere!

James 1:4 ~ "Let perseverance finish its work so that you may be mature and complete, not lacking anything."

*****Action Tool: Seek always the victories in your relationship with your mate. Take a moment each day to proclaim a victory that could not have been achieved without hope, trust, or perseverance.***

*****Action Step: Identify an area of your relationship where you find it difficult to maintain a mindset of hope or trust. Discuss with your mate why this is; and come up with an action step that you can do together to overcome this lack. Take a few minutes to journal the issue and the solution in the space below so that you can reference it in the future.***

****Extension Step: Following the same steps as above, identify a situation in your professional life where a lack of protection, hope, or trust is causing you to struggle in your ability to persevere in that situation. Find the appropriate time and place to address the person that you feel is keeping you from your goal. This conversation has to be delicate, especially if the other person is not in the same place in their walk with God as you are. Choose your words and your timing carefully!***

Study 2

Respect

A few keys to respect

Having a respect-filled relationship is one of the biggest challenges that face couples today. My wife and I are blessed to be mentored by some amazing people who have taught us what it truly means to respect one another. I am going to warn you now, some of this may not be easy to swallow as men, but I hope you take my words to heart. Now is probably a good time to get your ego in check and make sure your heart is open; and you are ready to receive some sharpening.

As a man, being disrespected by someone, especially someone you trust, is the fastest way to throw you off your Godly path. It can evoke in you, a stronger negative emotion and reaction, than any other form of distraction that the devil can send your way, including the temptation of other women. I've seen time and time again, Godly men who can turn their eyes in the presence of scantily clad women with ease. Those same men, when faced with a disrespectful coworker or family member, are bewildered or nearly enraged almost instantaneously.

As we go through this next section of the book, my intention is to outline some of the triggers and signs of disrespect; and show you how to diffuse those situations. It is also to show you your responsibilities as a Godly man and leader in the areas of respect with your mate, as well as everyone else in your life.

Something else to consider when dealing with issues of disrespect in your life is that you have to understand why you feel so disrespected. You then have to calmly communicate your strife to the person who you feel is being disrespectful. Everyone has a different perception of what is and what isn't respectful. We are all wired with a different personality type and we have all faced different life experiences. It's all of those experiences combined with your own unique personality that cause you to have a unique perception of respect. If you don't communicate your perception of what is and isn't respectful to the people in your life, there is no possible way they can know how to act around you!

We are once again, going to start with the relationship between you and your mate, and then extend out to the other areas of your life.

Put her in her place!

Yep, I said it. Your mate has to know where she stands in your relationship. Do you know where that place is? Let's look back to where it all started; the book of Genesis.

Genesis 2:22 ~ "Then the LORD God made a woman from the rib he had taken out of the man, and he brought her to the man."

Your mate's rightful place is at your side!

Woman was created from the rib of man. God did not create her from your heel, so she is not to be walked on. He did not take her from your spine, so she should not walk behind you. Woman was created to walk along side of and be "as one with man". Your wife is not your property; she is not less than you; she is your helpmate in life and she is your sister in Christ. Together you walk through life as one flesh before God. If you want your bride to respect you, take her out of the shadows and give her the rightful place she has at your side!

Genesis 2:24 ~ "That is why a man leaves his father and mother and is united to his wife, and they become one flesh."

***Action Tool: Your mate is your equal in every aspect of your life. She has unique skills and abilities that you don't possess as a man. See her differences and uniqueness as her strength; instead of as a weakness. Don't set yourself as the "bar" in your relationship. If two were to play that game, you'd fall short too!*

***Action Step: Identify 3 unique and amazing characteristics of your mate that she shines in and that you lack the same skill-set. Point out these things to her and be gracious for her differences.*

1.)

2.)

3.)

***Extension Step: Identify 2 people in your life other than your mate that you struggle in with in areas of respect. Are you making a point to embrace their unique differences and see them as an equal?*

1.)

2.)

It's all about submission!

This is one of the most misquoted passages from the Bible and it is absolutely infuriating to me when I hear it taken out of context. In Ephesians 5 it says "Now as the church submits to Christ, so also wives should submit to their husbands in everything.". Sadly, that's where many men choose to stop reading! Guys, listen to me, STOP IT! If you want your mate to submit you as she does the Lord, you have to do your part! Here's the rest of the passage:

[25] Husbands, love your wives, just as Christ loved the church and gave himself up for her [26]to make her holy, cleansing her by the washing with water through the word, [27] and to present her to himself as a radiant church, without stain or wrinkle or any other blemish, but holy and blameless. [28] In this same way, husbands ought to love their wives as their own bodies. He who loves his wife loves himself. [29] After all, no one ever hated their own body, but they feed and care for their body, just as Christ does the church—

I want you to take a moment to review that passage and really let it sink in. I'm not going to lie to you; that is a HUGE undertaking that God has put on us! You know why? Because it means you have to STEP UP! Do you really want your mate to be respectful and submit to your authority as the spiritual leader of the home? Then give her something worth respecting! You have to love her as Christ loved the church. Give yourself to her wholeheartedly and see her through Christ's eyes. Your job is to provide for her, to protect her, to pursue her daily.

"Your job is to make sure she knows that there is nothing of this earth that you wouldn't do to keep her safe."

Most importantly, you have to keep no record of wrong. If she makes a mistake, forgive her and let it go. You make mistakes every day, and God forgives you each time you ask. Forgive your wife, and present her to yourself as Christ did the church....without stain, or wrinkle, or blemish, but holy and blameless.

*****Action Tool:** How do you view the word submission? Your view and mindset is the single most influential factor on how you will approach every single aspect of your life! Therefore, if you change your mindset, you change your outlook! Don't view the act of being submissive as a sign of weakness or inferiority. View it as a characteristic of a loyal believer!*

***Action Step: What are 5 daily actions YOU can do to make your mate feel safe in your relationship? If she feels safe, she will be more comfortable submitting to you as the spiritual leader!*

1.)

2.)

3.)

4.)

5.)

****Extension Step: What are action steps YOU can take in other relationships in your life to demonstrate Godly leadership? I have listed a couple of verses to help you map these out.***

With your Children: Reference Ephesians 6:4 - "Fathers, do not exasperate your children; instead, bring them up in the training and instruction of the Lord."

1.)

2.)

In your professional life: Reference Ephesians 6:9 – "And masters, treat your slaves in the same way. Do not threaten them, since you know that he who is both their Master and yours is in heaven, and there is no favoritism with him."

(Note: Obviously, the employer/employee relationship isn't what it used to be in biblical times. I would highly recommend you avoid calling your boss "master" or your employees "slaves".) Regardless of titles, you are all brothers and sisters in Christ, treat them accordingly!

1.)

2.)

Another area of submission that needs to be addressed is our own submission to God as men. How can you expect your mate or anyone else to submit to your leadership if you are not showing them a proper example! Remember, it's not what is taught, but what is caught. Be a good example of a submissive spirit for the people who look to you for guidance.

Proverbs 3:6 ~ "in all your ways submit to him, and he will make your paths straight."

*****Action Step: What are 3 examples in your life of how YOU can be more submissive God in your life?***

1.)

2.)

3.)

***(Note:** If you're not sure what it looks like to be submissive to God in your life, don't worry, we will cover again later on in the purpose section of this book. If you can't fill in the answers now, come back to it when you find your answers!)*

Set the example!

Now that I have preached a bit, I want to clarify something. Do I think that as men, our wives deserve to be put on a pedestal above all others on this earth? To a point, yes. Does that mean you have to worship the ground she walks on? Absolutely not! The mere thought is foolish! The first commandment clearly states, "You shall have no other gods before me." -Exodus 20:3 Our job as men is to worship God and seek him in all we do. That is priority number one!

One of my wife and my favorite quotes, one that we have taught our daughters, and I hear my wife teach to other women is "Seek God so hard, that a man must go through Him to find you!" Guys, this is message is the same for us! Seek God first and with such a fever that your mate has no choice but to find you through Him! Show your mate that nothing else matters more that being a Godly man. Show your children that there is nothing more important than being a faithful servant to God. Prove to yourself that you are the man God called you to be.

I'm going to finish up this portion of the message with a word of caution. When you are in a relationship, you are not only responsible for yourself. You are responsible for the salvation, the protection, and the legacy of everyone in your home. It is your duty as man to set the best example possible. It is your duty to teach your children how a God's man should act. Don't act in any way towards your mate, a woman that is God's daughter, that you wouldn't accept another man doing to your own daughter. Let your family "catch you" being the REAL MAN that God has called you to be.

---

1 Corinthians 11:1 ~ "Follow my example, as I follow the example of Christ."

*****Action Tool: Follow the example of Christ. Walk through each action in your day as though your mate or your children were watching you. If you wouldn't do it in front of them, don't do it when they are not around!***

*****Action Step: What are 3 examples you are setting in your relationship with your mate that you wouldn't want her to reciprocate? Is it an anger issue, foul language, tone of voice? Choose 3 things you are ready to change in your life!***

1.)

2.)

3.)

*****Extension Step: Identify 3 characteristics in your professional or social life that need to be addressed. These might be the same as the ones with your mate. What 3 things do you do in your daily life do you do that you would consider to be a negative character trait of a potential "son in law"?***

1.)

2.)

3.)

The 3 P's of Respect!

The 3 P's of Respect is a concept that I learned not too long ago from a relationship enrichment training course held in Dallas, TX called "Creating Intimacy and Respect in your Relationship". Since attending the training, my wife and I have begun mentoring under the facilitator and his wife; and have begun teaching others the tools and techniques that we have learned. I would like to take this chance to give a special thank you to David and Amy Ensminger for their mentorship and teaching in our lives, and for allowing me to include these tools in this book. For more information about the training they offer, check the back of this book in the resources and tools section.

So, what are the 3 P's? Protect, Provide, and Pursue! These are 3 basic responsibilities you have as the man of the relationship, and as the leader of your home. If you are truly seeking to be a Godly man, and want your mate to respect you in your relationship, these are 3 critical areas you are going to have to get under control.

Protect

In dictionary.com, the word protect is defined as: "to defend or guard from attack, invasion, loss, annoyance, insult, etc; to cover or shield from injury or danger." This is a tall order for any man to fill. Remember when we discussed having to stand by your mate and walk through adversity together? Here is where the action step comes into play!

John 17:15 ~ "My prayer is not that you take them out of the world but that you protect them from the evil one."

Now, I know there are some of you men out there that are thinking to yourselves that this is not an issue, and that you would never let anyone near your mate or family. That's great! I was the same way for many years. Then, I was hit with a harsh reality. I was protecting my mate, my family, and my friends from everybody...........except me! There are few things in life as debilitating as realizing that you are the source of your family's feeling of insecurity! I soon discovered that I was not alone in this area. As I began to grow and understand my own shortcomings, I realized that the vast majority of men go through the exact same issues, for the exact same reasons I did. When you are home, your walls are down and YOU feel safe. There is nothing wrong with that within itself; you should feel safe in the confines of your own home. However, when a man let's his walls down, he tends to let all the frustrations of the day come to the surface. Sadly, it's his family that receives the brunt end of his frustrations as they surface. Bottom line, you have to protect others from you! When you are not being the protector, you are the offender. Where there is an offender, there is a lack of safety, which means a lack of trust. No relationship can survive without unwavering trust!

****Action Tool: Protection is all about safety. In any relationship in which you are the leader or role model, you will be completely ineffective if the other person doesn't feel safe.***

****Action Step: Find a quiet place to sit with your mate and ask them to identify the top 3 things you can do to make them feel safe in your relationship. Ask them what the characteristics of a protector are from their viewpoint.***

1.)

2.)

3.)

Extension Step: List 3 other people in your life that look up to you or consider you to be a person of leadership, role model, or mentor in their life. Find a moment this week to ask them if there are times when they don't feel like it's safe to communicate with you. There may not be anything, and if so, that's great!

1.)

2.)

3.)

Provide

Provide is a word that men commonly associate with money. Society has trained men that in order to be the "provider" of the home, they have to be the bread winner of the family. You go out, you work 40 or 50 hours a week (or more), and you then proceed to spend everything you make on a house, car, and whatever it takes to make the wife and kids happy. Ever heard the term "Happy wife, happy life"? Though it sounds good as a societal theory, it doesn't play out very well in the real world; and to be honest, what society says it takes to make a woman happy is really not as important to most women as you have been led to believe! Want to know the key flaw with society's theory of a "provider"? Society's theory assumes that all women are, by default, materialistic!

It's time for a reality check, guys. If you think that a big house and a six figure income is going to earn you the respect of your mate, your family, your friends, or your peers........you're wrong! I know this first hand, and can tell you that what society has taught us, as men, is misleading and destructive! Some of the most miserable years of my marriage were when I was making the most money! The sad part was, the unhappier I became, the more I pulled away from my family in order to go make more money. One of the hardest things I ever had to hear as a man, was my wife telling me "All the years you spent working yourself to death to be the provider you thought I wanted, I felt like I was living the life of a single mom."

During those times, I was almost never home, and when I was home my mind was somewhere else. The whole time, all my family wanted was for me to home and spend more time with them. Though I was "providing" a home, a new car, and all the worldly things they wanted, I wasn't providing for their real needs. My wife needed to see a man that was devoted to loving her and being there for her. My kids needed a father that spent time with them, invested in their daily lives, and showed them every day that they were more important than his work. Those are the qualities of a true "provider"!

I'll never forget the day these principles finally sank in. I was sitting in the back row of a business conference listening to a man named PJ McClure. When he was introduced as "The Mindset Maven" I chuckled and thought to myself, this should be interesting. I'd been through multiple self development trainings; what could this "business coach" possibly tell me that I haven't already heard. Two hours later, I found myself in the back of the room holding back tears. What he said that rocked me at my core was very simple. He simply asked:

"Are you someone who has built your life around your business, or your business around your life?" ~PJ McClure

If you want to be a true provider for your family and for everyone else that needs you, it's time to start focusing on providing them with what they need most: YOU.

Provide the people in your life with a loving and caring man of God that is dedicated to growing and developing them in the ways that God teaches in the Bible. Provide them with your time. We all get the same 86,400 seconds each day. No matter how much money you make, you can't buy more and you can never get back the ones that are lost or wasted. Think about these things as you work through this next action study.

*****Action Tool: Being the provider is all about leadership! If you want to earn and maintain respect from the people in your life, provide to them the one thing no other person on earth can give them, time with you!***

***Action Step: Time to dig deeper! Ask your mate what are the top 5 things that she needs you to provide; other than her basic daily needs. It's time to find out what her emotional and spiritual needs are from you as the leader of her home. Don't go surface level guys, your only cheating yourself if you do!*

1.)

2.)

3.)

4.)

5.)

***Extension Step: Take the rest of this page to journal what your definition of "provider" looked like in your life up to this point.*

Then, down below your first definition, write yourself a new "provider statement". In 10 words or less, write down your commitment to your mate, your kids, your family, or whoever you need to provide for. This definition is your commitment to yourself and one that is your responsibility to fulfill!

Pursue

Do you remember when you and your mate first started dating? You would go out of your way to spend time with her, show off for her, to make her smile. Whatever it took to get her attention.....you did it! By definition, (via dictionary.com), the word pursue means to "to strive to gain; seek to attain or accomplish". You spent days, weeks, months, maybe even years chasing her down and doing whatever it took to win her heart. Then, you got engaged, or married, and you stopped.

For men, the idea of pursuit is a specific task. It means the end goal is capture. You got her to fall in love with you; you got the ring on her finger, now your job is done. It's time to let your guard down and just be yourself. The problem with that is, that's not the guy she fell in love with!

Your mate fell in love with the guy who adored her; the guy who pampered her and gave in to her girlish whims. Now, just to be fair, I will say this; I know this is a two way street. As men, we are not the only ones who put our best foot forward at the start of a relationship; and, we are also not the only ones who have a tendency to change our habits once we get settled into a relationship. However, this study is not about your mate, it's about you. This is not the time to discuss all the things your mate does and try to justify your half-hearted efforts. Pointing fingers and playing the blame game will bring you nothing but arguments and fighting. There is not a single scenario in which playing the blame game ends well, so there no point in doing it to begin with!

So, what does pursuit have to do with respect? When you were pursuing your mate, i.e. courting or dating, she saw the side of you that put her needs first. It was your actions of selflessness that earned you her respect and the sense of safety and trust she needed to be comfortable with you. Those are the moments that she cherishes and can't get enough of. When you stopped chasing her, you started to tear away at that sense of safety and trust, which in turn, began the deterioration of the respect she had for you.

Here is the good news; you can get every single bit of that respect back and you can have a world of fun doing it! All you have to do is start pursuing her again. If she likes flowers, buy them for her. If she hates doing the dishes, do them for her. If she likes to dance, dance with her! Whatever it was that you used to do that made her smile and overflow with joy, that's what you need to start doing again. One of the most amazing night's I can remember having with my wife was taking the kids to our parents, coming home and cooking dinner together. Then, we cranked up the music and danced in the living room like we were kids. We didn't watch television, we didn't get sucked into social media sites; we just enjoyed spending time with each other. You don't have to go out and spend a bunch of money to pursue your mate; it can be a simple night of pampering her that makes all the difference in the world.

Now, there are a couple of issues of pursuit that need to be addressed before I send you off into your next action step and challenge. The first issue we have to address is your mindset moving forward. You have to stop viewing the pursuit of your mate as a goal to attain. It's not something you can put on your task list to do, and then just check off the list.

Think of pursuit from the perspective of a football coach pursuing a victory. Does the coach use the same set of four plays for every possession? Of course not! The other team would figure him out almost instantly! Your mate is the same way. You can't get settled into a routine of "if I do this, she'll do that". She will see right through it, and it will tell her that your motives for pursuit are not pure. Every day with your mate is like a new set of downs on the gridiron. You have to constantly make changes to your game plan and adjust to her needs, emotions, and even mood on any given day.

The second issue is a harsh reality check for many men; I know it was for me. That reality is: pursuing your mate does not start a six o'clock at night and is not about sex! Pursuing your mate starts the moment you wake up and has to be an all-day effort. By the way, when you do pursue your mate from sunup to sundown, it's still not about sex. It is about building and maintaining a deeper relationship with her. Did I mention that pursuit is not about sex? The bitter truth is that some days you are going to go above and beyond in every way and still end up lying in bed, listening to her snore and wondering what went wrong. To save you some sleepless moments, I'll just tell you the answer; nothing went wrong! She had a perfect day, is madly in love with you, and you still didn't get sex! Don't worry about it. If the only reason you are going out of your way to pursue her is so she will have sex with you, you're doing it for the wrong reasons! With that said, it's time for the challenge!

My challenge to you is to go pursue your mate! Chase her around the house, be a show off, be spontaneous, and do whatever it takes to get that girlish giggle out of her!

*****Action Tool: This one is very simple. Do whatever it takes to put the sparkle back in her eyes. Get her smiling, giggling, rolling her eyes at your antics; whatever you use to do back in the good ole days.......start doing it again!***

***Action Step: Ask your mate to tell you 3 things you "used to do" when you were dating that you don't do now. These are the silly goofy things you did that made her feel special. Write them down and make a point to start doing them again. Once you have these 3 back in the rotation, ask her for more!*

1.)

2.)

3.)

***Extension Tool: Think about pursuit in the areas of friendship and business. Remember, pursuit is about building and maintaining relationships. Ever had client you chased for months; then got the contract signed and now you hardly ever talk to them? Write down the names of a couple of people you invested a lot of time in when you first met, but now hardly ever speak to. Choose to recommit to your friendship and give them a call!*

Study 3

Understanding Godly Friendships

What is a Godly friendship?

Godly friendships are your true friends. These are the men, and on occasion women, in your life that want to see you succeed in every aspect of your life and are willing to help you get there. When a true friend helps you, and, they will if you ask them, they expect nothing in return except your loyalty and friendship. In Proverbs 17:17 it is written that ***"A friend loves at all times, and a brother is born for a time of adversity."*** God has put key men in your life to get you through your hardest times. They have been there all along, living life with you and waiting for you to activate and declare them as your true friend and fellow man of God. What most men are missing out on; is the declaration and activation of the friendship. Those key people that God has placed in your life are waiting for you tell them what a crucial role they play.

In general, men tend to be afraid of this kind of declaration. We spend our days in a corporate or entrepreneurial environment where we are constantly on the defense; and having to keep our guard up. In these environments, men are constantly competing for higher rank, better sales numbers, or more favor from management. These environments are like shark filled waters, or so it seems. That shark-tank environment is the mistaken impression that society has engrained in us. Society teaches us that we should always watch our back and don't trust anybody because they all want what you have and are willing to do whatever it takes to get it. With that kind of mentality, friendship within the workplace is often seen as a distraction or a sign of weakness. The man who tends to be the "socialite" is viewed as having ulterior motives. In all reality, he is probably the most secure and confident guy in the office. He knows who he is, what he is doing with his life, and just wants to enjoy his time with others. He talks to you because he is trying to declare a friendship!

Ok, don't get me wrong, I'm not saying the guy at the office that talks constantly and is incredibly annoying has been sent by God to be your best friend, but on the other hand, he could be. What we have to understand as men is that in order to find our true friends, we have to start communicating. Start looking at the men in your life that have been there beside you when you were struggling. That doesn't mean they necessarily volunteered to pull you out of the mud; it means they have always been there no matter what happened in your life.

So how do you declare the Godly friendships in your life? Start talking to them! If someone has played a significant role in your life and has impacted you in a positive way, you have to tell them the impact they have made! Then, you take time to invest in the relationship. You'll never keep true friends if you don't invest yourself in them.

A friendship between two people is a living manifestation of your relationship. Think about growing a friendship from the aspect of a farmer tending to his crops. If you don't nourish and care for crops on a daily basis, they will wither away and die. Your friendships are the same way!

Once you have declared what your friend means to you, it's time to see what you mean to them. One of the easiest ways to find out where your friendship stands with another man is to ask him to be your accountability partner for something. Not something that is a major struggle in your life, but something that is surface level. If he hesitates or gets put off by the question, you have your answer! He didn't even know what you were going to ask and is already looking for a way out. That's not a true friend! A true friend says "yes" to help you with your problem, and then asks what the problem is!

*****Action Tool: Declare your friendships! It's time to stop thinking that the men in your life know how you feel and what their friendship means to you. They'll never know if you don't tell them!***

****Action Step: Identify 5 men in your life that have stood beside you through the good and the bad. Once you have declared your friendship, you have to start investing in this friendship. Next to their name, write down at least one action you can take on a regular basis to invest in them.***

1.)

2.)

3.)

4.)

5.)

Going deep?

Why is isolation the number one problem that men face in their walk with God? The answer is simple; men don't want other men to know what's going on in their lives. The question is, why not? God call's us to have accountability partners and to seek strength in other men. Remember Proverbs 27:17? "As iron sharpens iron, so one person sharpens another." These men are in your life to sharpen you into the precision tool that God has intended.

In today's society though, as men, we have been taught that to admit we have problems will make us vulnerable, and to be vulnerable is to show weakness. For starters, the complete opposite is true. The ability to be vulnerable shows incredible strength and Godliness. When you are faithful to God's command, and you start surrounding yourself with the company of other Godly men, what you find is that as a group, your vulnerabilities begin to fade. When your deep seeded struggles are brought into the light, there is no opportunity for the enemy to hold these things against you any longer.

If being vulnerable and sharing your issues is the fast lane to overcoming the struggles, why is it so hard for us to do as men? The answer boils down to one word; trust. There is a prominent and well noted philosophy in sales that if you want people to spend money, they have to know, like, and trust you. That same concept applies to every other aspect of your life, especially friendship! Getting to know someone and even getting them to like you is easy. Getting them to trust you is a whole different ballgame. There are people in my life that I have known for years, but wouldn't share a single thought with them about my personal struggles. The reason is simple; I don't have a significant level of trust built with them to do so.

One of the issues that I see with many new and developing men's groups is that the men are not connecting within the small groups; they're not "going deep". When you take a look at the dynamic of these start up groups from an outsiders perspective, and incorporate the old sales philosophy of know, like, and trust, the problem seems to stick out like a sore thumb. You have groups of guys who don't know each other very well, aren't completely sure they like everybody in the group, and don't trust anyone at the table further than they can see them. Combine this with the added stress that they only meet once a week for a couple of hours and you have a recipe for disaster!

So, how do you break through this barrier of surface level friendships and start finding strength through vulnerability? First, you have to stop looking for deep connections in shallow water. If you are still warming up to the idea of being vulnerable with other men, or are new to men's groups in general, don't expect yourself or the other men at your table to just jump in with both feet and start sharing their inner most feelings. It's not going to happen for the overwhelming majority of men; and there is nothing wrong with that. For some of you, it may take weeks, months, or in some cases years before you feel that you are able to be fully vulnerable.

Before I go any further, I want to clarify something about that last statement. There are some men who have had such a traumatic past that their ability to trust anyone is incredibly difficult. Whether it is due to childhood abuse, cases of PTSD, or other sever trauma, they are just not going to open up without a long term proving period or divine intervention. What that afore mentioned statement is not, is your chance to hold back and pull away from the men in your life who are trying to sharpen you and help you in your walk with God.

Now, on the other end of the spectrum, there are a few exceptions to the general rule of tight lipped and stand offish tendencies. If you are someone who doesn't mind sharing everything in your heart with anybody who will listen, this is your chance to be the example for the other men in your life! Show them you are willing to be vulnerable and that you are safe. Show them you are trustworthy by trusting them.

For the rest of you, as my friend Bob Beaudine would say, "You go to your WHO!" Turn to your true friends who know you inside and out, the ones that have known you for years, and the ones you know you can trust. Turn to the men in your life that are Godly men and that you know won't lead you astray. These are the men that God has strategically put in your life to be there to hold you accountable and to strengthen you. All you have to do is ask them. Once you have developed your core group that you are comfortable being vulnerable with, you will find that you aren't as worried about sharing your issues with other men, such as those in your local men's ministry or small group, that you haven't known as long. When you have reached this point, it is then time to start being the example of vulnerability and strength to other men.

*****Action Tool: Vulnerable is strength, not weakness. Change your viewpoint, and you will change your willingness to go deep!***

*****Action Step: Remember the 5 men you listed in the last action step? These are the men in your life that you already have the potential to "go deep" with. Write each of their names again, and then list one area of your life that they have consistently been able to strengthen you.***

1.)

2.)

3.)

4.)

5.)

Knowing the "1"

In every man's life, there is one person who is above and beyond all others, they are your "1". This person is your best friend and is the one person that you can tell any and every deep dark secret in your life without fear of being judged, criticized, or shamed. Your best friend is the person that you want to share every day of your life with regardless of anything else that happens in your life. I believe and teach the 12-3-1 philosophy that is outlined in the book, *The Power of WHO*. (See resources section for more info on this book) Basically, you have twelve people in your inner circle of friends, three of the twelve are your closest friends, and of those three, one is your best friend. The "one" is the person that you have such a kindred heart-connection with that nothing can tear your relationship apart. When you fail to invest in this relationship, you feel like there is a part of you that is void. That is your "one". Please know, I am speaking of your earthly friendships. There should never be a point in your life that God is not at the forefront of your world.

To the married men

First, I am going to address the married men who are reading this. This message also applies to any of you who are engaged to be married. When you married your wife, you made a commitment to live with her, as one flesh, for the rest of your days here on earth. In the book of Genesis, it says: (Chapter 2, verse 23-24)

The man said, "This is now bone of my bones and flesh of my flesh; she shall be called 'woman,' for she was taken out of man."

That is why a man leaves his father and mother and is united to his wife, and they become one flesh.

She is a part of you now! When you took those vows, you took an oath of trust, truthfulness, encouragement, support, celibacy, and agreed to do it.....for as long as you both shall live. There is nowhere in the Bible that says you are as one flesh, except when....... It's just not there!

When you unite with your bride, it is a forever commitment to live life with her, as one, before God, till you take your last breath. She is your "one"! She absolutely has to be the closest and most trusted friend in your life, without exception! The minute you allow any other person to take that role in your life, you are betraying the commitment you made to her. Make a point to share your life with her every day and be sure she knows she is your one. Even within the confines of a marriage, you still have to declare your friendship with your mate. You have to solidify with her that you have put a value on your friendship that no other person on this earth can come close to.

One of the tools that Bryn and I have used over the years to deepen and declare our friendship and trust in each other is "the truth game". The truth game has very simple rules, and you can play it anytime, anywhere. Here's how it works. When you are struggling with a conflict or feel convicted to share something with your wife and are not sure how she will take it, you simply say the word "truth" to her. (I also use "truth" if I feel she is holding back from telling me something she isn't sure how I will respond.) If she is in a place to receive whatever it is you have to say, she in responds in kind by saying "truth" back to you. Then, you say what you need to say! If she is not in a place to receive it, she simply says not right now, and then lets you know when she ready to talk.

Now, there are a couple rules to playing the game. First, anything that is said in truth has to be the 100% complete truth without reservation. It doesn't matter how good or bad the "truth" is, you have to say it. Also, we don't use the truth game just for the bad stuff; if we did, neither of us would want to do it. We use it any time we want to know the raw emotions in each other heart. Because of this, it has become a staple of our lives, and something that we cherish.

The only other rule to the truth game is that whatever is said during that time stays in the confines of the time we are playing. Similar to the old saying about, "What happens in Vegas..."; the rule of the truth game is "what is said during truth, stays there". The truth game is a place of safety and nothing that is said during that time is allowed to be used against each other or held over each other's head once it's done. Regardless of the topic that is discussed, it is dealt with, the appropriate measures are taken to put it to rest, and then the both of you agree to move on and not bring it up anymore. That is not to say that there won't be the occasional fall out or additional time of rebuilding needed if you are discussing tough matters; what it says is that you and your mate agree not to allow the matter at hand to put a wedge in your relationship. This is the tool we used when I finally came clean with my wife that I had had two affairs in the early part of our marriage. Conversely, it is the same tool I use to find out where she really wants to go on date night or on vacation and she doesn't think it's something I would want to do. The "truth game" has been an invaluable tool in my life and has brought my relationship and friendship with my bride to a level that is unrivaled by any other relationship in my life.

*****Action Tool: Incorporate "The Truth Game" into your relationship with your mate. Stick closely to the rules until you feel comfortable, and then make up your own rules so that it is a custom fit for your relationship.***

*****Action Step: For the next 14 days, make it a priority to use the truth game to learn something new about your mate. Remember, games are designed to be fun, don't just use it when you need to make a confession!***

To the single men

Now, to those of you who have yet to make a lifelong commitment: the "one", for right now at least, should be a man in your life that you have a true heart-connection with. For some, it may be your father, grandfather, uncle, cousin, or other close relative. For others, it may be a childhood friend that you still talk to almost daily. Regardless of the kinship, as a single man your best friend is the person who invests in your world consistently. I say "a man" because having a woman as your "one" before marriage can and will create what's known as "soul ties". The topic of soul ties, and the difficulty in breaking them, is a complete study within itself and one that I am not going to cover in this book.

Your best friend is someone who has been at your side to console you when you didn't think things could get any worse; and was there at your side when life couldn't be better. Anything less than this is unacceptable. Your best friend will never intentionally lead you down the wrong path or try to sway you from God's word. Instead, they are the one who is encouraging you to seek the Lord in your time of troubles and are there to pray with you and guide you when needed.

*****Action Tool: It's time to declare your "one". Hopefully, you already have this person's name written down as one of your five in the "going deep" exercise. If you don't have the ability to go deep with your best friend and trust them with your inner most goings on, chances are they really aren't your best friend!***

****Action Step: Write down the name of your best friend in the space below, and then journal a short entry describing what they have done in your life to earn the title of being your best friend.***

Study 4

Suiting up for Battle

Taking the next step

The first three sections of this book have been about addressing your relationships with the people in your world. Once you have declared, solidified, and strengthened those relationships, it is time start embracing the rest of the world and begin to fulfill the great commission, outlined in Matthew 28: 19-20, that has been instilled in every believer.

"Therefore go and make disciples of all nations, baptizing them in the name of the Father and of the Son and of the Holy Spirit and teaching them to obey everything I have commanded you. And surely I am with you always, to the very end of the age."(NIV)

Before you can go out and fulfill this ultimate calling that is in your heart, there are two key elements that you need to understand. The first, which we will discuss in this section of the book, is to understand the elements and application of the armor of God. The armor of God is your defense against the enemy when you are going out into the world to do God's work. The second element, which will be discussed in section five, is the discovery and awakening of your specific purpose in God's kingdom. So, what is the armor of God and how do we apply it to the modern world that we are living in? Let's first look at the passage that outlines this armor, and then we will break down the passage into individual actions just as we did in previous sections.

The Armor of God (Ephesians 6:10-20 NIV)

10 Finally, be strong in the Lord and in his mighty
power. 11 Put on the full armor of God, so that you can take
your stand against the devil's schemes. 12 For our struggle
is not against flesh and blood, but against the rulers,
against the authorities, against the powers of this dark
world and against the spiritual forces of evil in the
heavenly realms. 13 Therefore put on the full armor of God,
so that when the day of evil comes, you may be able to
stand your ground, and after you have done everything, to
stand. 14 Stand firm then, with the belt of truth buckled
around your waist, with the breastplate of righteousness in
place, 15 and with your feet fitted with the readiness that
comes from the gospel of peace. 16 In addition to all this,
take up the shield of faith, with which you can extinguish
all the flaming arrows of the evil one. 17 Take the helmet of
salvation and the sword of the Spirit, which is the word of
God.

18 And pray in the Spirit on all occasions with all kinds of
prayers and requests. With this in mind, be alert and
always keep on praying for all the Lord's people. 19 Pray
also for me, that whenever I speak, words may be given me
so that I will fearlessly make known the mystery of the
gospel, 20 for which I am an ambassador in chains. Pray
that I may declare it fearlessly, as I should.

Belt of truth

The first element to the armor of God is the belt of truth. We have discussed matters of truth and honesty multiple times in this book because they are such a vital component of living a Godly life. If it were not such a vital tool, the word truth would not have been referenced almost a hundred and forty times in the Bible.

Wearing the belt of truth in today's society can be accomplished through living what is commonly known as a "transparent" lifestyle. Transparent, by definition, means that light is able to pass through you. In John 8:12, Jesus says,

"I am the light of the world. Whoever follows me will never walk in darkness, but will have the light of life."

There is a clear and repeating theme in the Bible that describes the ways that are good as light and the ways that are evil as darkness. To be transparent means that you allow the light (good) to pass through you in all directions, which in turn, leaves no room for darkness (evil) to dwell within you. Living a transparent life means quite simply that nothing is hidden within you. You've pulled all the skeletons out of the closet and you don't hide in the mistakes of your past. In order to live this type of transparent lifestyle, you have to have the relationships in place that have already been discussed. There has to be people in your life that have you are willing to go deep with and share with them any and all of the hurts, hang-ups, struggles that you are facing in your adult life. If you are not willing to do this, you are allowing the enemy an opportunity to shadow your world in darkness and begin to isolate areas of your life in which you need the most help.

****Action Tool: Look at the belt of truth as a transparent window to your life. For every aspect of your life that you are not willing to share with someone, you are effectively placing a "smudge" of darkness on your belt. These smudges are weaknesses in your armor and are open gates for the enemy to enter into your life and do his bidding.***

****Action Step: What are your smudges? Not the surface level smudges that can be resolved with a quick talk with the Lord, I am talking about the deep seeded secrets that you have been holding on to and carrying around for years. If you expect the belt of truth to do its job in protecting you, you have to make sure there are is no damage in the armor! Take the next page to journal some of the things in your life where darkness still resides. Then, call it into the light and remove the enemy's hold against you by praying for God to show you full grace and forgiveness once and for all, and then share your struggle with someone in your life that you can trust. Once it's out in the open, it can be held against you no longer!***

The breastplate of righteousness

When you think of the breastplate of righteousness, what comes to mind? Let's break down the term itself to see exactly what it is and how we apply it to our role as a man of God.

Is the breastplate a small piece of armor? Of course not! The breastplate is designed to cover your entire upper torso where all of your vital organs reside, including the Spirit of God within you. Your breastplate is the largest and most encompassing piece of armor you can wear.

How about righteousness? Righteous is defined as (dictionary.com) "acting in an upright, moral way; virtuous". A moral way is quite simply acknowledging and recognizing the difference between right and wrong, and standing up for what is right. The "right", in this case, is the law of God.

When you put the terms back together, the breastplate of righteousness is the armor that protects your inner spirit and all that is vital to you so long as your actions are in accordance with the laws of God. To have the breastplate of righteousness in place means that you are following the word of God precisely; and abiding in the laws that He has set forth for you in your life. When you are doing this, you are protected from the slanders and scorns that will be aimed specifically at your Godly spirit.

One of the struggles that will diminish the effectiveness of this piece of your armor is the tendency in men to become self-righteousness. Being self-righteous is a form of pride. We discussed pride in the first section of this book, but I want to visit this topic again for just a brief moment. When you become self-righteous, you have effectively put your own virtue and moral way above that of God's. This is recognized easily when you look at the successes of your life that you have begun to take credit for. In revelation 3:17, it says *"You say, 'I am rich; I have acquired wealth and do not need a thing.' But you do not realize that you are wretched, pitiful, poor, blind and naked"*. Being self-righteous is the act of retaking the reigns of your life and placing God in the passenger seat. Once you have done this, you are not humble and are no longer abiding in the righteous of the Lord. God can't protect you when you do this!

*****Action Tool: In order to wear the breastplate of righteousness, you have to give God the reigns in every aspect of your life. When you try to control the situations in your life or take credit for any of the blessings that have been bestowed upon you, you are allowing pride to run rampant and you are now vulnerable to the enemy's attack on your spirit.***

***Action Step: Identify 3 areas of your life that you habitually find yourself saying, "I got this". These are the areas of your life that you are so confident in what you do, that you find yourself not seeking God's intervention and wisdom before you make decisions. Remember, pride comes before the fall. Get rid of the pride now and put God's righteousness back at the helm before your success becomes your stumbling block!*

1.)

2.)

3.)

Godly foot-ware: readiness and peace

How do you walk *"with your feet fitted with the readiness that comes from the gospel of peace"?* Having your feet fitted in readiness means that, as a warrior for God, you have your guard up against evil at all times. Have you ever heard the phrase, "I'll get all the sleep I need when I'm dead"? Long before Sam Elliot said it in the movie "Roadhouse", that saying had been around for many years, and there is no clear record of when it was first used. However, the quote is really not as much of a cliché as you may have thought. In Isaiah 57:2, he writes *"Those who walk uprightly enter into peace; they find rest as they lie in death."* Our work as men of God is will never be done until we take our last breath here on earth. Only when the Lord finally calls us home to His kingdom; we are allowed to rest. As warriors for the army of God, we are to be ready for battle at any and every moment of our life.

Having readiness or being ready for something literally means to be completely prepared or equipped for immediate action. To have our feet fitted with readiness is our calling, as Godly men, to be prepared to fulfill our greater calling and commission at any given moment, regardless of what is going on around us. God's timing and need for us is not dictated by our earthly schedule and there is no snooze button when God's alarm goes off!

The gospel of peace is living your life in the fulfillment of God's word. When you are obeying God's law and are firm in holding true to the teachings of the Bible, there is an overwhelming sense of contentment and confidence that will overcome you. Carrying the gospel of peace is walking in harmony with God.

When you are contemplating or are in the act of doing an action that is not in harmony with God's law, you know it. That feeling you get when you are out of harmony with God is commonly known as a guilty conscience. The Bible speaks repeatedly to us to keep a clear conscience, and the only way to do that is to repent of your sins and to keep nothing in your life pent up that you can feel guilty about. Remember the belt of truth and the life of transparency? I promise you, there is a correlation between these two elements. When your life is transparent, and you steadily repent when you sin, there is no room in your spirit for guilt, which in turn, will keep you in the state of peace you are seeking.

*****Action Tool*: Open your heart to hear the calling of God and be ready when he calls. As one of God's warriors, your duty is to be ready to answer His call at all times and to seek Him daily for his calling in your life.**

***Action Step: A guilty conscience is the easiest way to be unprepared or unready to do God's work. Keeping an open heart and a clear conscience at all times must be a priority! Take the rest of this page and the next to journal anything in your life right now that is weighing on your conscience. It may be something recent; it may be something from a long time ago. Once you are done journaling, repent for the things that are holding your peace captive and ask the Lord to show you what it is that you need to do to put an end to your guilt once and for all.*

Helmet of salvation

The helmet of salvation is your deliverance and protection from the penalties of sin! When you wear the helmet of salvation, you are surrendering your life and your human nature to God's will. In numerous instances in the Bible, it tells us to be clothed and rejoice in His salvation in our lives. Salvation on this earth through Christ is our protection. He is our savior; our protector from the harm of our enemies. When we fail to wear the helmet of salvation, our mind is an open door to the suggestions of the world. If you look back to the fall of man, all the way back in Genesis, Satan did not force Eve to eat the apple, nor did Eve force Adam. All it took was the power of suggestion from the serpent! The hardest obstacle for almost any man is to believe his own salvation in his mind. That is why your armor of salvation is the helmet; it is there to protect your mind and your thoughts!

To help you get a clear understanding of this, let's break it down a bit. You know what a helmet is, so let's focus on salvation and what it really means to accept your salvation in your mind.

Trying to live your life as a Godly man in today's world is hard enough on its own merits. We live in a time and a society that provides temptations in so many different ways and at such a rapid pace that it is difficult to live your life in a way that honors God. There are outlets of sin and temptation available today that the men of biblical days didn't have to face. With that said, as men of God in today's world, we have to develop and utilize the tools we have at our disposal now that the men of the Bible didn't have. The most powerful tool you have to guard your mind in today's world is to understand why your mind works the way it does. You have to truly dig down and understand and bring to the surface the struggles you face and ask yourself why you face them. The answer in most cases has to do with actions caught and lessons learned as a young boy.

Just as doctors do in the medical field, as men we have to seek the cause or root source of our struggles, not just try to treat the symptoms. Take addiction as an example. For several years, I personally struggled with drug addiction. It wasn't the drug that I wanted; it was the feeling of being in control. As a child, I lived with a father who very controlling over me and I always felt like I was on a leash. The drugs gave me a false sense of control over things in my life. Once I faced my own demons and issues with my dad, and turned control of my life over to God, drugs had no appeal to me.

Another very common issue with men is their struggle with masturbation. In case you haven't already figured it out guys, struggles with masturbation and sexual temptation are not just a simple struggle with the need to ejaculate. There is an underlying emotional struggle in your life, for whatever reason, that you believe is being soothed by the act of masturbating. The reality is, it doesn't work, and that's why you feel guilty after doing it! You have to figure out what the feeling or emotion is that you are hiding from before you can overcome the battle in your mind. You can throw out your entire porn collection and lock down your computers so tight that you can barely access your email, but those things are just a band-aid and you will still end up losing the battle of masturbation if you don't start dealing with and understanding what the underlying emotions are that you are suppressing.

What I want you to do now is take an assessment of your own mind and the thoughts that captivate it. What are your struggles? Is it pornography, addiction, self-worth, acceptance? What are the roadblocks of self-doubt and insignificance in your own mind that are keeping you from truly accepting and walking in your own spiritual salvation? For many of you, this is going to be a very difficult exercise. The question is, do you want to wear your helmet of salvation and stand confident in the salvation you have through Christ or will you choose to leave yourself unprotected? To go out into the world with your helmet of salvation on, is to walk through the day with the same level of confidence in yourself that Christ has in you! He already knows the kind of warrior you are, He is waiting on you to believe it!

***Action Tool: When you feel yourself struggling with a battle of your mind, seize the thought and ask yourself "why do I".....want to do this, feel this way, etc. Identify the root emotion that is causing you to have that thought or want to do that action. Once you have the root discovered, pray for God to deliver you from it! One thought a time; you will win your confidence and strengthen your armor!*

***Action Step: What is it in your life right now that is challenging your confidence in your salvation? These are the areas of your life that you feel "not good enough" or "unworthy" in. As sons of God, and brothers in Christ, we are heirs to our Heavenly father's throne! We are worthy to receive all that is in God's kingdom, we just have to believe it! Take the next page to journal your struggles in salvation and then map out the root cause of each. Use these understandings as tools to overcome your feelings of doubt.*

Shield of faith

In verse 16, Paul writes, *"In addition to all this, take up the shield of faith, with which you can extinguish all the flaming arrows of the evil one."* Having faith in the teachings and promises of God's word are a powerful weapon against the enemy. Notice how Paul says you can extinguish ALL the flaming arrows of the evil one with your faith. When you are truly walking in faith, though you may be tested, there is not a single weapon the enemy has against you that can harm you! One of my favorite passages about being faithful is found in Psalm 4: 2-3:

How long will you people turn my glory into shame? How long will you love delusions and seek false gods? Know that the LORD has set apart his faithful servant for himself; the LORD hears when I call to him. (NIV)

Those are the words of a Godly warrior! Having an unwavering faith in God is better than having your own personal red phone to the president!

How amazing and empowered would you feel as a man if you knew without question that when you prayed, God was listening? Would you still be saying the simple prayers of "bless this food" and "watch over my family"; or would your prayer life be something so much more? When you have the shield of faith acting in full force in your life, you are powerful!

Many have said that the sword of the spirit is your only offensive weapon; I believe that the shield of faith is where God's armor over you turns the tide from defensive armor to offensive armor. Think back to the days of the Roman army or even to knights in the medieval times. Their shield wasn't just to block their opponent's advances; it had a dual purpose as a short range offensive weapon. One swift backhand blow from a shield can weaken the defenses of your enemy.

Not only can your shield of faith block the long range weapons of the enemy; it can also be your act of force to remove close threats! Men of God, stand tall in your faith and press forward against the enemy's threats!

*****Action Tool: Learn to use your shield of faith as the dual purpose armor that it is. Let it not only protect you from the enemy's advances in your life; use it to gain ground for the kingdom of God!***

****Action Step: Where your faith is unstable, so is your armor! Look at the areas of your life that your faith tends to buckle easily. Identify and list 3 areas of your life where your faith is most frequently shaken. Then, write out your plan of action to solidify and strengthen your faith in these areas. (Note: This is a good opportunity to utilize your inner circle of accountability partners!)***

1.)

2.)

3.)

The sword of the spirit

The sword of the spirit is the word of God; aka your Bible, or nowadays, your Bible app. Your strongest and most effective way to be an offensive weapon for the kingdom of God is by spending time with the Lord every single day and reading your Bible! Just as you had to study and read the books your teachers assigned you in school, you have to study and spend time reading God's word. This is by far the one elements of being a man of God that I see the majority of men struggling with.

Why is it such a struggle for so many men? It comes down to two things: priorities and discipline. Remember when I told about how I had to turn my way of thinking around from putting my professional life before my family life? The same was true about my daily agenda and my spiritual growth. I wanted to spend time with the Lord, but I lacked the discipline to do so.

Up until about a year ago, my days were so hectic that the only way I could make time for God without taking away from the other daily activities that I found to be of value was to get up earlier in the morning. I am not typically a morning person and getting up earlier wasn't an option. It was my own selfishness keeping me from giving God his time every day. My sword at that time was about as effective as trying to chop wood with a butter knife! I knew the fundamentals of God's teachings, I learned a new one every weekend, but didn't realize that fundamentals are only the tip of the iceberg. You can't just show up at church on Sunday and expect the pastor to give you enough sharpening to last you all week. That's not his job! The pastor's job is to guide you through a fundamental teaching and give you just enough information so that you will leave there and be ready to spend time digging in to the word and understanding how that fundamental can be applied into your life. Stop expecting the pastors of your churches to do your job for you! That's laziness!

In order to give your sword the precision sharpening it deserves, you have to develop a strong sense of discipline and be willing to make sacrifices in your life. If you give God the first part of your day, he will multiply that time back into your life. When I made the decision to stop being selfish, and start spending the first hour of my day with God; and with my wife as a couple before God, it completely changed the way I looked at my day. When I made it a point to start my day by sharpening my sword, overcoming the struggles of the day came with less effort. I'm not saying I don't still struggle; the struggles I face now are just different. However, the viewpoint from which I look at those struggles is different, also.

Once you make the decision to be empowered and become an offensive weapon for the Lord, your outlook on spending time with God will change. Once you make that shift in your mind, you begin to view the Lord as the ally that you strategize with each morning. He is the five star general that you look to each morning for your daily battle plans.

***Action Tool: Make the choice to sharpen your sword daily! Be disciplined and choose a time of day that you know you can be with the Lord without distraction. For some, this may not be first thing in the morning, and that's ok.*

***Action Step: Take this page to outline your daily schedule. It's time to make your daily devotional study a priority and start sharpening your sword every day. If you have never made daily time with God a priority, I suggest you start with 15 minutes a day. Then, work your way up to whatever amount of time God is putting on your heart to spend with him. There is no wrong answer here; if you ask him, God will share with you how much time he wants you to spend with him each day.*

The power of prayer

The final passage that Paul writes after he outlines the armor of God is in verses 18-20. It is a message about prayer and a personal prayer request for him. Though prayer isn't typically recognized as a part of God's armor, it is included under the same sub heading in most Bibles. I think that Paul's teaching about when to pray and praying his prayer for ourselves; as men of God, is a powerful tool that can strengthen our armor. The first part of the passage is:

And pray in the Spirit on all occasions with all kinds of prayers and requests. With this in mind, be alert and always keep on praying for all the Lord's people.

Just as you have to make time each day to study the word, you should also make it a point to spend time in prayer. Pray for yourself, your brothers and sisters in Christ, and for all of those that have asked you for prayer. One thing I want to challenge each of you to do is to pray BIG and to pray repeatedly for the blessings that you want God to bring you in your life.

The first part of that is to pray BIG! As an heir to the kingdom of God, you have all of God's blessings at your disposal. The problem is, you don't ask for them! Lord, bless this food. Lord, protect my family. Lord, give me enough money to pay my bills. Do you wonder why you struggle with living a mediocre life? It's because that's all you ever pray for! Stop spending all your prayer time praying for the menial things in life that He is going to do anyway! Go for the big stuff and believe that God is going to give it to you.

The second part of the challenge is to pray repeatedly. I remember listening to a message by Andy Stanley in which he made the reference that God isn't Fedex. You can't just submit your prayer order on Monday and get your blessing delivered on Thursday. It just doesn't work that way! You have to be precise, consistent, and persistent in your prayer. Keep praying until God is so overwhelmed by your repeated prayer that he answers you just to shut you up!

*****Action Tool: Pray BIG and Pray with persistence!***

*****Action Step: Write down your top 3 BIG prayers and start praying for them every day. Ask yourself, "What are three things in my life that I know aren't going to happen unless God intervenes?" Those are the prayers you need to write down.***

The second part of the passage Paul writes is a prayer for him. In verses 19-20, it says:

Pray also for me, that whenever I speak, words may be given me so that I will fearlessly make known the mystery of the gospel, for which I am an ambassador in chains. Pray that I may declare it fearlessly, as I should.

If you read the words of Paul's prayer carefully, you will see that this prayer is specifically designed for God's warriors! As men of God, we go out into the world to do God's work and we ask that our words be the words from the spirit; we pray that the words we speak and profess are spoken out of our own bindings to God's teaching; and we pray that when we speak, we speak confidently, and that we allow God's will to be done through us! All of these elements are in Paul's prayer!

*****Action Tool: Pray for the Holy Spirit to fill you and that God's words flow through you each time to minister to another man.***

*****Action Step: Rewrite Paul's prayer so that it becomes your personal prayer to God each time you set out to do God's work. Memorize this prayer and be disciplined to say your prayer each time you set out to do a specific work for God.***

[illegible] the passage [illegible] it says.

[illegible] that what [illegible] will become [illegible] it impossible [illegible]

[illegible] prayer [illegible] carefully [illegible]

[illegible] God's word [illegible] we pray that [illegible] that we [illegible] will to be [illegible]

[illegible] God's word [illegible] through [illegible] ment.

[illegible] personal [illegible] God [illegible] God's word. Memorise this prayer and be disciplined to [illegible]

Study 5

Awakening your Godly Purpose

Recognizing the great commission

We are all called to do the Lord's work and to spread his message throughout the world. One of the repeating patterns in men of God is the inability to recognize the great commission without becoming overwhelmed. Let's take a look at Christ's words to the disciples, found in Matthew 28: 18-20.

Then Jesus came to them and said, "All authority in heaven and on earth has been given to me. Therefore go and make disciples of all nations, baptizing them in the name of the Father and of the Son and of the Holy Spirit, and teaching them to obey everything I have commanded you. And surely I am with you always, to the very end of the age."

Christ's calling to us as followers and believers, is quite simply to go out into the world and spread his message. Where the majority of men become frozen in their walk is at this simple request. When Christ says for us to "go and make disciples of all nations" it isn't necessarily a literal translation to every man that follows him. When Christ spoke those words to the disciples, he was telling them as a collective unit of followers. God has given us the gift of the Holy Spirit to be our guide on earth and is God's spirit within us all. In that, each of us has been given a specific and unique commission from God while we are here.

Among the men of God that I have worked with, there is one word within the entire scripture that is like kryptonite to Superman; it's the word "go". "Go" is the action word of the great commission. If you have made it to this point in book, hopefully you have begun to see that the whole point of this book is to encourage and empower men to become men of action in every aspect of their lives and in every relationship they are a part of. If you want your life to be pleasing the Lord, you have to be a man of action!

As we dive into this final section of the book, I am going to ask you to dig deep and to really focus on God's specific and unique purpose for your life. Discovering and implementing God's purpose for you in your life will be the turning point in your ability to become the man of action that God has called you to be.

Acknowledge your Calling

Not too long ago, I had a conversation with a friend of mine who was struggling with answering the calling that God had put on his heart. He knew the specific calling of the Lord in his life, and knew what he was supposed to be doing. However, he has spent the past fifteen years in a profession that does not allow him to pursue his calling. For many men, this case of career vs calling is a constant struggle that is like a plague on their soul. Just like my friend, they know what God has called them to do, but are stuck in the rut of their career choice or specific training. There has to come a point in a man's life when he makes the decision to do what God has called him to do. I'm not saying you need quit your job and jump into whatever it is that is weighing on your heart. On the other hand, I can't in good conscience tell you not to, because that's exactly what I did. By trade, I am not a writer; I am not a public speaker; and I certainly am not a men's pastor! However, I know what God has asked me to do and I am a firm believer that God does not call the qualified, he qualifies the called!

What is it in your heart that God is calling you to do? From what I have seen and studied in men throughout my life, the ones who are living in their calling are the ones that are finding success in almost every area of their lives. What sets them apart from the masses is their willingness to turn over the reign of their life to Christ and allow His work to be done through them rather than allow their specific training be the construct of their ability.

"From the east I summon a bird of prey; from a far-off land, a man to fulfill my purpose. What I have said, that I will bring about; what I have planned, that I will do." Isaiah 46:11

One of the key elements to understanding your own calling from God is to realize that God's purpose will be achieved with or without you. You see, God does not need us in order for his will to be done, yet, he wants us. If we, as men, are unwilling to follow the specific calling that he has placed in our hearts to do during our time here on earth, he will find someone else who is willing, and he will make them abundantly able to do it! Acknowledging your calling is telling God, "I am ready, I am willing, and through your means I will be made able!"

*****Action Tool: If you are called, you are already qualified! Stop worrying about the criticisms of earthly judgment and do what God is asking you to do. Answering your calling is an act of Faith!***

***Action Step: It's time to really dig deep and look at what God has called you do for Him. What is the task or the mission that God has put on your heart to do? For many, this is an area of your life where things come so naturally to you, you do them without a second thought. Take this time to journal out your specific calling from God and describe what it looks like, feels like, and how you would feel as a man of God if you were doing it. You shouldn't have to think about it; if it is your calling, you will be able to visualize it with abundant clarity!*

Defining your specific purpose

There is a distinct difference between purpose and calling. The calling that God has put on your heart is the "what" of the equation. Your calling is the description of your mission in life as a servant to the Lord, what your purpose looks like in action. Your purpose on the other hand, is the "why". Helping people uncover and unlock the "why" in their lives is, for me, living out my own "what"! My specific purpose, or my "why", is simply "awakening Godly purpose". When I am given the opportunity to speak into the lives of others and be the vessel of the Lord that allows them to unleash God's purpose for them in their lives; I am not only actively living on purpose for myself, I am helping others achieve their potential!

One common reaction that men have when they recognize their calling is an exasperated "You want me to do what?" Followed shortly with "Why me, Lord"? The good news is that you're not alone. These same questions were asked by some of the greatest leaders from the Bible! Let's look at one example, a conversation between God and Moses, taken from Exodus 3:11-14.

11 *But Moses said to God, "Who am I that I should go to Pharaoh and bring the Israelites out of Egypt?"*

12 *And God said, "I will be with you. And this will be the sign to you that it is I who have sent you: When you*

have brought the people out of Egypt, you will worship God on this mountain."

13 *Moses said to God, "Suppose I go to the Israelites and say to them, 'The God of your fathers has sent me to you,' and they ask me, 'What is his name?' Then what shall I tell them?"*

14 *God said to Moses, "I AM WHO I AM. This is what you are to say to the Israelites: 'I AM has sent me to you.'"*

The answer to the "why me, Lord" question is not complicated. You do it because that is what God has asked of you! You don't need to worry yourself with what anyone else thinks about your calling or wonder how you are going to get it done. When you are walking the path that God has chosen for you, the means to accomplish your calling will be given to you at the appropriate time.

In Proverbs 19:21, Solomon writes: *"Many are the plans in a person's heart, but it is the LORD's purpose that prevails."* As faithful servants to the Lord, we have to be willing to put aside our own wants and earthly desires in order see what God wants to do with our lives. In order to do that, we have to be living a life that allows our purpose for ourselves, to be God's purpose for us. You needn't look any further than that to discover the true meaning of life! When you dedicate your life to fulfilling God's plan for you, your life here on earth takes on a whole new level of meaning.

Remember, you are already qualified because you have been called. The "why me, Lord" is because that is what He ask told you to do. Defining your Godly purpose is putting into words what God needs you to do to fulfill the calling he has put on your heart. The words the Lord gives you to define your purpose will become your purpose statement. Your purpose statement is not going to be something that is long and drawn out; it will be short and to the point. When you discover it, the words will resonate within your spirit. Now, it's time to do some more work and see if you can define your specific purpose.

*****Action Tool: Your Godly purpose statement is the definition of what empowers you to fulfill your calling. These are the words that when you say them, it makes the hair on your neck stand on end. That feeling is the Holy Spirit rising up within you!***

*****Action Step: What is the specific purpose statement that defines your life? Knowing the "why" that describes your calling is essential to fulfilling your mission here on earth. Remember, God has already told you to do this, all you have to do is put it into words!***

To discover your own specific purpose, start journaling about the mission God has put on your heart. You may start out with an entire paragraph, and there is nothing wrong with that. Once you have it all down, start condensing it down until it is one sentence or less. Don't forget; your calling is what your purpose looks like; your purpose is what drives you to fulfill your calling!

Proclaiming your Godly mission

To awaken the empowerment and drive that comes with knowing God's specific purpose for you in your life, you have to be able to envision the culmination of your purpose statement and your calling. When you combine your specific "what" and your specific "why", your action plan becomes overwhelmingly clear. To paraphrase a quote I heard from one of my mentors and advisors, Scott Schilling, "When the what and the why are big enough, the how just shows up!" The great news is, your calling and your purpose are always big enough! Why? Because they were put on your heart directly from God!

When you break into the realm of walking through your days actively seeking to fulfill God's calling on your life, there is a sense of contentment in the road ahead. The road ahead of you may be rough and riddled with confrontation, but you are confident that God is going to see you through to other side. In Proverbs 20:5, it says: ***"The purposes of a person's heart are deep waters, but one who has insight draws them out."***

Your Godly mission stays dormant inside you until the point in your life when you decide to take action on it. Long before you ever took your first breath, back when God was knitting you inside your mother's womb, he engrained in you a mission, for his kingdom, only you were meant to fulfill. The question is: will you make the choice to fulfill it? For this last action step, I want you to take what you have been journaling in the last two exercises and combine them into your Godly mission statement. This statement is your action step and your daily encouragement as you set out to fulfill what God has put in your heart to do for his kingdom. When you are faced with adversity, this is the statement you can come back to remind you of what you have been put on this earth to do! It's your oath to God and to yourself! To give you an idea of what it may look like, I will give you mine as an example.

My specific Godly mission statement: To empower and encourage men with abusive or addictive backgrounds through awakening Godly purpose in their lives.

*****Action Step: Write your Godly mission statement, and then start living it!***

ADDITONAL RESOURCES

Below are just a few of the books and trainings that have had heaviest influence on me in my walk not only with God, but in life. I encourage you to read, attend or utilize as many of these resources as you can to further you in your studies.

The Power of WHO! *Written by Bob Beaudine*
www.powerofwho.com
The Power of WHO Is the definitive guide to understanding friendships! There is no doubt why this book is a NY Times best seller! ~SRT

Flip the S.WI.T.C.H! *Written by PJ McClure*
www.themindsetmaven.com
When you read this book, your mind will truly *Flip the S.W.I.T.C.H!* PJ McClure has mastered the art of teaching you to re- train your mind and thought process, focus on the important things in life, and get more accomplished! ~SRT

SOS at Zac's Ridge (Experiential based life training)
www.sosinc.org

Creating Intimacy and Respect in your Relationship
www.creatingintimacyandrespect.com

[illegible] just a few [illegible] book [illegible] have [illegible] fluence on me [illegible] with [illegible] affect yo[illegible] [illegible] as you can [illegible] further [illegible]

[illegible] Written by [illegible]

The Power of WHO [illegible] definitive [illegible] [illegible] There is no doubt who [illegible] best [illegible]

[illegible] Written by PJ McClure

[illegible] read this book your mind will [illegible] mastered [illegible] process [illegible] accomplished [illegible]

[illegible]

www.ingramcontent.com/pod-product-compliance
Lightning Source LLC
Chambersburg PA
CBHW071005040426
42443CB00007B/676
* 9 7 8 0 9 7 5 3 9 3 6 5 9 *